STUART THOMAS
Peace on Earth
Reflective Services for Advent to Epiphany

Kevin
Mayhew

First published in 1996 by
KEVIN MAYHEW LTD
Rattlesden
Bury St Edmunds
Suffolk IP30 0SZ

0 1 2 3 4 5 6 7 8 9

ISBN 0 86209 862 9
Catalogue No 1500062

Front cover: *The Nativity* from *The Hours of Etienne Chevalier*
by Jean Fouquet (c. 1425-1480).
Bridgeman Art Library/British Library, London.

Cover design by Veronica Ward and Graham Johnstone
Typesetting by Louise Hill
Printed and bound in Great Britain.

Contents

Contents

Introduction

The arrival of Jesus Christ on this earth two thousand years ago was hardly the most spectacular event of all time. Centuries earlier he had been described by the prophet Isaiah as the 'Prince of Peace', and his birth was announced by the angels with the words 'Glory to God in the highest, and on earth peace to people on whom his favour rests'. But, apart from some shepherds out in the fields and a group of eastern astrologers, few took any notice of it, and it was in the stillness and peace that the Creator God took human form to become part of his own creation. Despite the whirlwind of activity into which we're drawn at Christmas, we only recognise the presence of the Prince of Peace in our lives when we stop rushing about for a while and give him time to fill our hearts with his peace. Carol services and family events abound in our churches at Christmas, and while these are very commendable, they're also quite busy and active. There's a need for a liturgy which isn't too formal or informal and enables us to step aside from the busyness and discover the peace which Jesus came to bring.

The six services in this booklet are all fairly short and mostly participative, one for each of the four Sundays in Advent, and one each for Christmastide and Epiphany. There is space for silence and quiet meditation based on the ASB themes and readings for each week, but the action which might come from this is also highlighted. The hymns suggested are all taken from the New Anglican Edition of *Hymns Old & New* (Kevin Mayhew 1996), but are mostly widely available in other collections. Worship leaders may find other songs are equally suitable. Those selected here reflect the quieter, more thoughtful tone of the services.

These services are intended to provide not only an alternative liturgy, but more importantly to enable worshippers to see more of the significance of the Incarnation and be drawn as a result deeper into the love and grace of God as we see it revealed in Jesus Christ.

STUART THOMAS

Advent Sunday

Leader   The Lord our God is King. We come before him to offer our worship, to give him thanks and praise, and to acknowledge his kingship over our lives. He alone is worthy to receive glory and honour and to him alone we bow.

Silence

Leader   Almighty God, you are King of kings and Lord of lords. Every knee must bow before you in worship and adoration. Receive our praises and prayers, poor and unworthy as they seem to us, and, as we come before you now, help us to know your kingdom reigning within our hearts for your name's sake. Amen.

SONG   *Heaven shall not wait* (Iona Community)

Leader   The Herald comes to bring good news and announce prosperity saying:

All   The Lord our God is King!

Leader   The watchmen on the city wall lift up their voices in jubilation, saying:

All   The Lord our God is returning to Zion!

Leader   The ruins of Jerusalem break out in triumphant songs, saying:

All   The Lord our God has saved his people!

Leader   How lovely on the mountain are the feet of the Herald who brings good news of salvation and restoration!

All   From one end of the world to the other all nations will see the deliverance of our God!

READING   The King will say to those on his right, 'Come, you who are
Matthew 25:34-40   blessed by my Father; take your inheritance, the kingdom prepared for you since the creation of the world. For I was hungry and you gave me something to eat, I was thirsty and you gave me something to drink, I was a stranger and you

invited me in, I needed clothes and you clothed me, I was sick and you looked after me, I was in prison and you came to visit me.'

Then the righteous will answer him, 'Lord, when did we see you hungry and feed you, or thirsty and give you something to drink? When did we see you a stranger and invite you in, or needing clothes and clothe you? When did we see you sick or in prison and go to visit you?'

The King will reply, 'I tell you the truth, whatever you did for one of the least of these brothers of mine, you did for me.'

MEDITATION   Think of all the people you met last week. Your neighbours, your friends, your family . . . the postman, the shop assistant, the traffic warden . . . the proud, the difficult, the self-centred . . . the joyful, the humble, the caring. Think about the words you spoke. Were they sensitively chosen or hastily blurted out? Think about the love you offered. Was it freely given or selfishly held back? How would you be able to recognise Christ in all these people? Ask God to open your eyes to his presence in the world; to open your lips to share his message; to open your heart to receive and share his love.

Leader   King of the Nations, we stand before your throne of judgement. You know our every thought and attitude, our every action and reaction. We can hide nothing from your searching gaze.

Leader   We confess that we have been careless in word and deed.

All   Lord, forgive and restore us.

Leader   We confess that we have failed to see you in the poor and needy.

All   Lord, forgive and restore us.

Leader   We confess that we have selfishly pursued our own ends rather than seeking your will.

All   Lord, forgive and restore us.

Silence

Leader   The King says, 'You have my Father's blessing, for you fed me when I was hungry; you gave me drink when I was thirsty; you took me in when I had nowhere to go; you clothed me when I was naked; you visited me when I was ill and in prison.'

Group A   Lord, help us to recognise the hungry in this world – those deprived of nourishment by human selfishness and greed. May we and all Christian people work to overcome exploitation and bring dignity and hope to those in need.

Group B   Lord, help us to bring refreshment to those who thirst for righteousness, hope and freedom from fear. May we and all Christian people work to establish justice and peace in our world.

A   Lord, help us to give comfort and shelter to the homeless, the refugee and those who feel they belong nowhere. May we and all Christian people show them your welcoming arms and provide a place where they can belong.

B   Lord, help us to see the needs of the poor and destitute with your compassionate eyes. May we and all Christian people work to alleviate their distress and provide them with the necessities of life.

A   Lord, help us to care for those who are sick in body, mind and spirit. May we and all Christian people bring your healing touch to all whose lives are spoiled through illness, infirmity or mental torment.

B   Lord, help us not to forget prisoners, especially those whose present captivity is the result of injustice or political corruption. May we and all Christian people work tirelessly for justice and proclaim that the Lord releases captives.

Leader   The King says, 'You have my Father's blessing. Come and enter the kingdom which has been made ready for you.'

SONG   *I, the Lord of Sea and sky (Here I am, Lord)* (Dan Schutte)

Leader   Let us keep silence as we pray for our world and those in all kinds of need.

Silence

Leader   Rejoicing in the hope set before us, we pray as Jesus has taught us, saying:

All   Our Father . . .

Leader   As we leave this place to do your will,

All   may we love you more deeply, worship you more joyfully, follow you more closely and serve you more wholeheartedly, until one day we see you face to face, Jesus, our coming King. Amen.

Leader   Let us bless the Lord.

All   Thanks be to God.

Second Sunday in Advent

Leader   The Word of the Lord is living and active. Sharper even than a sword with two edges, it cuts through our defences and masks, exposing our inmost thoughts and attitudes, laying them bare before God's all-seeing eye.

Silence

Leader   Almighty God, you have given us your written word that through it we might encounter the Living Word, your Son Jesus Christ, our Saviour. As we come into your presence now, may we meet with him both through the Scriptures and in our own hearts, and receive his transforming power into our lives, for the sake of your kingdom. Amen.

SONG   *Open our eyes, Lord* (Robert Cull)

Leader   The Lord promises his people:

Group A   Come, you who are thirsty, and fetch water; come, you who have no food, buy corn and eat.

Group B   Come and buy, but not with money and not for a price.

A   Come and listen to me, and you will enjoy the fat of the land.

B   Come and hear me, and you shall have life.

Leader   The Lord says to his people:

A   I will make a new covenant with you to last for ever, to love you faithfully.

B   Nations you do not know will come running to you because the Lord has glorified you.

A   Let the wicked abandon their ways and evil people their thoughts.

B   Let them return to the Lord, who will have pity on them and freely forgive.

A   For my thoughts are not your thoughts, and my ways are not your ways.

B   As the heavens are higher than the earth, so are my ways higher than your ways, and my thoughts higher than your thoughts.

Leader   As rain and snow come down from heaven, and do not return until they have watered the earth, making it blossom and bear fruit, so shall the words of the Lord prevail. They will not return fruitless, but accomplish their purpose and succeed in the task he has given them.

READING
Luke 4:14-21

Jesus returned to Galilee in the power of the Spirit, and news about him spread through the whole countryside. He taught in their synagogues and everyone praised him. He went to Nazareth, where he had been brought up, and on the Sabbath day he went into the synagogue, as was his custom. And he stood up to read. The scroll of the prophet Isaiah was handed to him. Unrolling it he found the place where it is written: 'The Spirit of the Lord is on me, because he has anointed me to preach good news to the poor. He has sent me to proclaim freedom for the prisoners and recovery of sight for the blind, to release the oppressed, to proclaim the year of the Lord's favour.' Then he rolled up the scroll, gave it back to the attendant and sat down. The eyes of everyone in the synagogue were fastened on him, and he began by saying to them, 'Today this scripture is fulfilled in your hearing.'

MEDITATION

Consider the impact God's word has on your life. Is it there just to provide comfort and peace at moments of crisis and stress? Does it serve only to prove us right? Do we have a few favourite passages or are we open to the whole counsel of God? How do we respond when it confronts our prejudices and preconceived ideas? How do we react when it cuts into the comfort of our present lives and challenges us to live more for God's kingdom? Ask God to make you more ready to hear and receive his word, more open to its message and more willing to obey its instructions.

Leader   We open our hearts and minds to the Spirit of the Lord saying, may we be not only hearers of your word:

All   make us doers also.

Leader   When we read the Scriptures and listen to your voice in the stillness of our hearts, may we be not only hearers of your word:

All   make us doers also.

Leader   When we read your law and study your commandments, may we be not only hearers of your word:

All   make us doers also.

Leader   When we read the prophets and take in their message of repentance and obedience, may we be not only hearers of your word:

All   make us doers also.

Leader   When we read of the Early Church and understand their vision and commitment, may we be not only hearers of your word.

All   Make us doers also.

Leader   When we read of Jesus and his love for the poor, the exploited and the unloved, may we be not only hearers of your word:

All   make us doers also, so that your word is fulfilled and your kingdom built, for your name's sake. Amen.

SONG   *Love is his word* (Luke Connaughton/Anthony Milner)

Leader   Let us keep silence as we think of the poor, the prisoners, the blind and the oppressed, and allow God's compassion for them to be seen in us.

Silence

Leader   As we hear your word, may we act on it in our daily lives. The Spirit of the Lord is upon us in bringing the good news of God's kingdom to the poor and needy:

All   may we fulfil your word.

Leader   In proclaiming that those in captivity will be set free,

All   may we fulfil your word.

Leader   In announcing that the blind will have their sight restored,

All   may we fulfil your word.

Leader   In releasing those held in bonds of oppression,

All   may we fulfil your word.

Leader   In telling everyone that this is the time of the Lord's favour,

All   may we fulfil your word.

Silence

Leader   Following the teaching of Jesus, we pray as he taught us, saying:

All   Our Father . . .

Leader   As we leave this place to do your will,

All   may we who have heard your word learn what it teaches, take it into our hearts, and apply it to our daily lives, for in serving you will we find perfect freedom. This we ask for your name's sake. Amen.

Leader   Let us bless the Lord.

All   Thanks be to God.

Third Sunday in Advent

Leader   When the Lord comes he will banish all darkness, revealing the deepest secrets of our hearts. We can hide nothing from him, for he knows everything. Let us prepare ourselves to meet with him in worship.

Silence

Leader   Almighty God, we stand before you now as our judge, recognising our own unworthiness. Nothing we have done or could possibly do would make us worthy to come into your presence. Yet we stand before you too as our loving Father, who longs for us to respond to his gracious call. As we reach out to you, touch us with your gentle hand, enfold us in your strong arms and reassure us of your love, for your name's sake. Amen.

SONG   *Inspired by love and anger* (Iona Community)

Leader   The Lord says: Go up to a high mountain and announce the good news,

All   the Lord our God will come with great power.

Leader   Lift up your voice with strength,

All   the Lord our God will come to bring justice.

Leader   Take the good news to the city,

All   the Lord our God will come to bring salvation.

Leader   Speak tenderly to God's people,

All   the Lord our God will come to bring comfort.

Leader   The Lord says: Do not be afraid, but lift up your voice, for I will make a straight path through the desert; I will make every hill and mountain low; and I will make the rough places smooth and level.

All   The glory of the Lord will be revealed to all people and they will see it together.

READING
John 1:19-27

This was John's testimony when the Jews of Jerusalem sent priests and Levites to ask him who he was. He did not fail to confess, but confessed freely, 'I am not the Christ.' They asked him, 'Then who are you? Are you Elijah?' He said, 'I am not.' 'Are you the Prophet?' He answered, 'No.' Finally they said, 'Who are you? Give us an answer to take back to those who sent us. What do you say about yourself?' John replied in the words of Isaiah the prophet: 'I am the voice of one calling in the desert, "Make straight the way for the Lord".' Now some Pharisees who had been sent questioned him, 'Why then do you baptise if you are not the Christ, nor Elijah, nor the Prophet?' 'I baptise with water,' John replied, 'but among you stands one you do not know. He is the one who comes after me, the thongs of whose sandals I am not worthy to untie.'

MEDITATION

Who do the people around you think Jesus was – a good man, a great teacher, a guru, or God's Son? What impression have they got of him? Do they recognise him as being alive today? Do they think he can influence or transform their lives? What impression would they get of him from us? Have we been changed by God enough for anyone to notice? John the Baptist's role was not to draw attention to himself but to prepare the way for Jesus. Does our worship and service of God point people to his Son? Ask God to show us how we can 'prepare the way' for Jesus to come into people's lives.

Leader   We prepare for the coming of Jesus into our lives as Prophet, Priest and King, saying: Come to our hearts, Lord Jesus:

All   we make room for you there.

Group A   Come to us as Prophet to challenge our complacency and renew our zeal for you.

Group B   Cleanse and purify us from all that defiles, and make us ready to say, Lord, here am I, send me.

A   Come to us as Priest to stand by us in our weakness, and enable us to stand in the presence of God.

B   Give us confidence to approach the throne of grace to receive mercy and help in our time of need.

A	Come to us as King to reign in our hearts and lives, and give us strength to live as members of your kingdom.
B	Strengthen us to uphold your laws and to bring your justice and righteousness to the world around.
Leader	Come to our hearts, Lord Jesus:
All	we make room for you there.

SONG   *When God Almighty came to earth (God on earth)*
(Iona Community)

Leader	In the quiet of our hearts we ask God to reveal to us those situations in which we can 'prepare the way' for him to enter and bring his gentle rule of peace and love.

Silence

Leader	As we leave this place to return to our homes,
All	may your kingdom come in our hearts.
Leader	As we go to our workplace and colleagues,
All	may your kingdom come in our service.
Leader	As we live among our families and friends,
All	may your kingdom come in our relationships.
Leader	As we mix with people in the everyday tasks of life,
All	may your kingdom come in our lives.
Leader	Looking for the coming of God's kingdom, we say together:
All	Our Father . . .
Leader	In our home and family
All	let us bless the Lord
Leader	In our work and leisure
All	let us bless the Lord
Leader	In our worship and devotion let us bless the Lord.
All	Thanks be to God.

Fourth Sunday in Advent

Leader   The angel said to Mary, 'Do not be afraid, for God is pleased with you. You will give birth to a son who will be called Jesus. He will be great, and God will give him the throne of David. His kingdom will never end.' Mary responded, 'Let it be to me according to your word.'

Silence

Leader   Almighty God, Creator of the universe and Lord of all, with you nothing is impossible. You fashioned the earth out of nothing and all things depend on you for life, yet you chose to become part of your creation. Open our eyes and hearts, we pray, to your mighty power, your gracious humility and your unending love, and help us to respond in glad obedience, for your name's sake. Amen.

SONG   *For Mary, mother of our Lord* (John Raphael Peacey)

Leader   A shoot starts to grow from the stump of Jesse and a branch from its roots. The Spirit of the Lord is resting upon him.

Group A   A Spirit of wisdom and understanding; a Spirit of counsel and power;

Group B   a Spirit of knowledge and the fear of the Lord.

Leader   When he comes, he will not pass judgement on what he sees or hears;

A   he will judge the needy with righteousness and decide in favour of the poor;

B   he will destroy the wicked with a word from his lips.

Leader   On that day the wolf and the lamb will live together, and the leopard will sleep by the goat;

A   a little child will lead the calf and the lion together, and the young of the bear and the cow will play with one another;

B   the child will play near poisonous snakes and come to no harm;

All the whole earth will be filled with the knowledge of the Lord as the waters cover the sea.

READING
Luke 1:26-38a

In the sixth month, God sent the angel Gabriel to Nazareth, a town in Galilee, to a virgin pledged to be married to a man named Joseph, a descendant of David. The virgin's name was Mary. The angel went to her and said, 'Greetings, you who are highly favoured! The Lord is with you.' Mary was greatly troubled at his words and wondered what kind of greeting this might be. But the angel said to her, 'Do not be afraid, Mary, you have found favour with God. You will be with child and give birth to a son, and you are to give him the name Jesus. He will be great and will be called the Son of the Most High. The Lord God will give him the throne of his father David, and he will reign over the house of Jacob for ever; his kingdom will never end.' 'How will this be,' asked Mary, 'since I am a virgin?' The angel answered, 'The Holy Spirit will come upon you, and the power of the Most High shall overshadow you. So the holy one to be born will be called the Son of God. Even Elizabeth your relative is going to have a child in her old age, and she who was said to be barren is in her sixth month. For nothing is impossible with God.' 'I am the Lord's servant,' Mary answered. 'May it be to me as you have said.'

MEDITATION

Mary's decision to accept God's will and obey him was costly and demanding. She was probably a simple country girl who neither expected nor demanded much out of life. Quite content to remain in Nazareth and live in happy domesticity, Gabriel's appearance must not only have scared her but filled her with fear about her future. No doubt she was looking forward to her impending marriage to the local carpenter, so explaining her pregnancy to him would be a major problem, while her reputation in the community could be damaged too. Most of all, Mary suddenly found herself at the centre of God's plans. Her obedience was crucial if his divine will was to be fulfilled. She could have made many excuses, but instead willingly accepted the personal and practical problems of having her first child for the sake of serving God. What sort of excuses do we make for not obeying God? 'It doesn't make sense'; 'God doesn't work like that';'What about my family, my career, my friends?'; 'People will think I've gone mad?' Are we prepared to accept the cost of following God's way so that he can fulfil his purposes through us? Ask God to help you avoid making excuses for not following his ways, to give us strength to face our fears and accept the cost of doing so.

Leader   Heavenly Father, we are tempted to find all kinds of reasons for not responding to your voice and obeying your will. When we worry more about our reputation than about your commission, make us loyal to you:

All   may your will be done in us.

Leader   When we consider personal convenience more important than willing service, make us faithful to you:

All   may your will be done in us.

Leader   When we allow fear of consequences to overcome our desire to serve you, make us confident in you:

All   may your will be done in us.

Leader   When we become so distracted by this world's crises that we forget our heavenly calling, make us committed to you:

All   may your will be done in us for the sake of your eternal kingdom. Amen.

SONG   *Lord Jesus Christ (Living Lord)* (Patrick Appleford)

Leader   As we keep silence together, let us bring before God those situations that seem difficult, threatening or impossible, asking him to accomplish his word in them.

Silence

Leader   When tasks threaten to overwhelm us and duties burden us down,

All   make us willing to follow your call.

Leader   When frustration and trouble drain us of energy and enthusiasm,

All   make us willing to obey your call.

Leader When conflict and opposition fill us with fear and tempt us to run away,

All make us willing to obey your call.

Leader When the concerns of this life blur our vision of your kingdom,

All make us willing to obey your call.

Leader Rejoicing in God's presence among us, we pray as our Saviour taught us:

All Our Father . . .

Leader As we leave this place,

All may we hear your voice.

Leader As we return to our homes,

All may we obey your will and serve you faithfully for no reward other than hearing you say, 'Well done, good and faithful servant.' Amen.

Leader Let us bless the Lord.

All Thanks be to God.

First Sunday after Christmas

Leader   At the time he had appointed, God sent his Son, born of a woman and born under the law, to purchase freedom for those who are subject to the law, so that they might receive the full rights and status of children. We are no longer slaves but children, and therefore also heirs, because of what God has done.

Silence

Leader   Almighty God, you are the Maker and Ruler of all creation and on you all life depends. Yet your Son Jesus Christ came to this world as one of us, to share our earthly life and by his death enable us to share your eternal life. As we see him, the Word made flesh, dwelling among us, may we also see his glory, the glory of the Father's only Son, and bow before him in worship and adoration, our Saviour and King. Amen.

SONG   *Cloth for the cradle* (Iona Community)

Leader   Dear friends, love comes from God so let us love one another.

Group A   Everyone who loves is born of God and knows him.

Group B   Anyone who does not love cannot know God, because God is love.

A   God's love for us was revealed when God sent his Son into the world so that we could have life through him.

B   Not our love for God, but his love for us in sending his Son to be the sacrifice that takes away our sins.

A   Since God has loved us so much we should love one another.

B   If we love one another, God will live in us and his love will be complete in us.

READING
John 1:14-18   The Word became flesh and lived for a while among us. We have seen his glory, the glory of the one and only Son who came from the Father, full of grace and truth. John testifies

concerning him. He cries out, saying, 'This was he of whom I said, "He who comes after me has surpassed me because he was before me."' From the fullness of his grace we have all received one blessing after another. For the law was given through Moses; grace and truth came through Jesus Christ. No-one has ever seen God, but God the only Son, who is at the Father's side, has made him known.

MEDITATION   Many great artists have attempted over the years to depict the Incarnation on canvas. Magnificent as some of their efforts are, they also tend to be fairly predictable: a silent, contented baby, his mother looking remarkably peaceful and unharrassed, Joseph watching benignly, and an assortment of farmyard animals behaving with unexpected decorum. Jesus' birth has been sanitised to make it acceptable and comfortable but as a result we miss its real impact and fail to ask the most important questions. Why did God choose such an inconvenient and obscure place and time for the birth of his Son? Why did he go to such lengths to enter into human experience? What do we see when we look at the manger – a symbol of ideal humanity; a normal baby who grew up to be one of the most remarkable people of all time; or God coming alongside us and entering human history in order to redeem humankind and transform our lives? The Incarnation wasn't sentimental or dramatic. Far from it. It was uncomfortable, inconvenient and at the time noticed by very few people. Its impact lies not in its circumstances but in its meaning for humankind. What significance does the Word made flesh hold for us? Ask God to make us more receptive to his Word so that its impact is seen in our lives day by day.

Leader   We rejoice at the coming of our Saviour in humility and lowliness saying, Emmanuel, God with us,

All   be born in us today.

Leader   We rejoice with the prophets who foretold the birth of the Messiah who would save people from their sins. Emmanuel, God with us,

All   be born in us today.

Leader   We rejoice with the shepherds who first saw the infant Jesus who would bring joy to the hearts of many. Emmanuel, God with us,

All   be born in us today.

Leader   We rejoice with the wise men who followed the star to find the new-born King who would be the Shepherd of his people. Emmanuel, God with us,

All   be born in us today.

Leader   We rejoice with the angels and the whole company of heaven at the birth of God's own Son, who is the Word made flesh. Emmanuel, God with us,

All   be born in us today.

Leader   We rejoice with all God's people at this time of celebration for the birth of Jesus, who ever lives to be our Saviour and Friend. Emmanuel, God with us,

All   be born in us today, and live in us until that day when we see you as you are, Jesus our Lord and King. Amen.

SONG   *Born in the night, Mary's child* (Geoffrey Ainger)

Leader   In a few moments of silence we think on the wonder of what God has done in Christ and pray that for his sake, other people may see him at work in our lives and be drawn into praise and worship, and faith in his mighty power and loving purposes.

Silence

Leader   In the world of nature around us

All   may we behold your glory.

Leader   In our work and relaxation

All   may we behold your glory.

Leader   In our worship and our service

All   may we behold your glory.

Leader   In times of enjoyment and sadness

All   may we behold your glory.

Leader   In one another and in people around

All   may we behold your glory.

Leader   As we celebrate the Word made flesh, we pray together as he taught us:

All   Our Father . . .

Leader   For Jesus, God's living Word,

All   let us bless the Lord.

Leader   For Jesus, the true Light who shines in the darkness,

All   let us bless the Lord.

Leader   For Jesus, the Father's only Son, full of grace and truth,

All   let us bless the Lord. Thanks be to God. Amen.

Epiphany

Leader   The prophet Malachi spoke of the fulfilment of God's word when he said: 'My name will be great among the nations, from the rising to the setting of the sun.' May we glimpse his glory and receive his power to preach the Gospel to all nations.

Silence

Leader   Almighty God, who in your Son Jesus Christ revealed your glory to all people, you have called us to be your faithful servants. Strengthen us by your Spirit, that in working for justice and peace we may uphold your name, and in proclaiming your good news of salvation may bring the light of your glory into the darkness of the world, for your name's sake. Amen.

SONG   *Within our darkest night* (Taizé Community)

Leader   The Lord says of his servant: 'Here is my servant who I uphold, my chosen one in whom I delight.

All   My Spirit is upon him, and he will bring justice to the nations.

Leader   He will not shout or raise his voice, or make himself heard in a public way;

All   he will never break the bruised reed, nor snuff out the smouldering wick.

Leader   He will faithfully bring forth justice;

All   he will neither falter nor be discouraged until he establishes his justice on earth.'

Leader   The Lord has created all that is and given life to everything on the earth;

All   he has called us in righteousness and taken us by the hand,

Leader   to be a beacon for the nations and a light for all people,

All   to open blind eyes, and bring out the captives from the darkness of their prison.

READING
Matthew 2:1-12

After Jesus was born in Bethlehem in Judea, during the time of King Herod, Magi from the east came to Jerusalem and asked, 'Where is the one who has been born King of the Jews? We saw his star in the east and have come to worship him.' When King Herod heard this he was disturbed, and all Jerusalem with him. When he had called together all the people's chief priests and teachers of the law, he asked them where the Christ was to be born. 'In Bethlehem in Judea,' they replied, 'for this is what the prophet has written: "But you, Bethlehem, in the land of Judah, are by no means least among the rulers of Judah; for out of you will come a ruler who will be the shepherd of my people Israel."' Then Herod called the Magi secretly and found out from them the exact time the star had appeared. He sent them to Bethlehem and said, 'Go and make a careful search for the child. As soon as you find him report to me, so that I too may go and worship him.' After they had heard the King they went on their way, and the star they had seen in the east went ahead of them until it stopped over the place where the child was. When they saw the star they were overjoyed. On coming to the house, they saw the child with his mother Mary, and they bowed down and worshipped him. Then they opened their treasures and presented him with gifts of gold and of incense and of myrrh. And having been warned in a dream not to go back to Herod, they returned to their country by another route.

MEDITATION

King Herod was a frightened, insecure man. He could assert his power only by putting on a show of self-importance and destroying anything or anyone that stood in his way. The contrast with the new-born King of the Jews is striking. Never do we see Jesus asserting himself over others or promoting his public image. He had little to do with the authorities and preferred to spend most of his ministry with the poor and oppressed, the broken and humble, foreigners and outcasts. As he hung on the cross at the climax of that ministry, the ascription over him read: 'The King of the Jews'. His reign is one of justice and peace; his rule is gentle and compassionate; his power serves to encourage and build up; in his kingdom there is no place for arrogance and self-assertion. This is the kingdom he came to reveal to all humankind. Is it revealed in our behaviour, or do we become destructive when we see our status under threat? Is it seen in our attitudes to the weak and exploited, or are we more determined to preserve our own lifestyle? Does it shine through our conversation, our actions and reactions, our deeply held views, or does the way we live and speak obscure God's glory to other people? Ask God to transform our attitudes, our conversations and our behaviour, so that by the way we live we reveal his glory to those around us.

Leader We kneel before Jesus, the King of kings, recognising that we do so not by our own merits but by his grace. We offer to him our lives in worship and adoration. Lord Jesus, we bring to you our gifts and offerings:

All accept and use them for your glory.

Group A We bring our personalities and temperaments;

Group B we bring our experiences and insights:

All accept and use them for your glory.

A We bring our abilities and skills;

B we bring our resources and possessions:

All accept and use them for your glory.

A We bring our knowledge and understanding;

B we bring our intuition and discernment:

All accept and use them for your glory.

A We bring our hopes and joys;

B we bring our fears and uncertainties:

All accept and use them for your glory.

A We bring the things we most want to keep hold of;

B we bring the things we are most afraid to lose:

All accept and use them for your glory, that you may be revealed to those among whom we live and work. Amen.

SONG *From the Sun's rising* (Graham Kendrick)

Leader As the glory of God, revealed in his Son Jesus Christ, shines in our hearts, let us keep silence and bring before him the darkness around us in the world which he seeks to dispel.

Silence

Leader   Heavenly Father, the light of your love shines in the midst of the darkness, chasing the shadows of gloom and despair. Help us to show your glory to the world.

Group A   Show your glory to the homeless and refugee, that they may find in you their eternal home.

Group B   Shine in the darkness of the poor and deprived, that they may know the riches of your grace.

A   Show your glory to the oppressed and exploited, that they may find in you true freedom.

B   Shine in the darkness of the victims of violence and abuse, that they may know your peace which passes all understanding.

A   Show your glory to the anxious and fearful, that they may find in you release from their troubles.

B   Shine in the darkness of the depressed and despairing, that they may know the joy of your salvation.

A   Show your glory to the sick and suffering, that they may find in you healing and wholeness.

B   Shine in the darkness of the dying and bereaved, that they may know the hope of your risen life.

All   May your love shine through us to bring the light of Jesus' love to the dark places of the world and disperse the shadows of evil and fear to bring glory to your name. Amen.

All   Our Father in heaven . . .

Leader   For the glory of God revealed in Creation,

All   let us bless the Lord.

Leader   For the glory of God revealed in his Son,

All   let us bless the Lord.

Leader   For the glory of God revealed by his Spirit, let us bless the Lord.

All   Thanks be to God.